SUPEI

Letting Go oi

MW01680973

Helping Black Women Break Free from the Superwoman Role

Ashley Alridge

Copyright

Published by:

Ashley Alridge

ISBN: 979-8-90417-628-0

Printed in the United States of America

Dedication

This book is dedicated to every woman who has been everything to everyone.

I see you, sis.

And I'm giving you permission to remove your cape.

Foreword

In a world that often demands us to be the backbone of our families, friends, and communities, the essence of simply being a woman can sometimes feel lost in the fray. "SUPERWOMAN" serves as a poignant reminder that while strength is a virtue, vulnerability is equally powerful. This book invites you to pause, reflect, and reclaim your identity beyond the roles that have defined you.

The heartfelt words presented here resonate deeply with many of us. They highlight the struggle of being the one everyone turns to, the fixer, the problem solver, the unwavering source of support. Yet, in this journey of self-discovery, we must ask ourselves: when was the last time we allowed ourselves to rest, to revel in our femininity, and to embrace the beauty of simply being ourselves?

As you dive into the pages of "SUPERWOMAN," you will find encouragement to shed the burdens that weigh heavily on your shoulders. This book is not just a collection of words; it is an invitation to reconnect with your true self, a Black woman who deserves to be soft, catered to, and free to breathe.

Together, we will explore the complexity of our identities, the weight of our responsibilities, and the profound strength that lies in embracing our vulnerability. This journey is not walked alone; it's shared, and we will support one another every step of the way.

So, let's embark on this journey of rediscovery. Let's reclaim our softness, our joy, and our right to simply be. Because you are not just a superwoman, you are a woman deserving of care, love, and rest.

Welcome to "SUPERWOMAN."

—Nakeitha Ross

Table of Contents

Introduction

Sis, That Cape Is Heavy

You were never meant to carry it all.

Friend, let's sit here for a moment.

When was the last time you allowed yourself to simply be a woman?

Not someone's wife.
Not somebody's mama.

Just a Black woman.

A Black woman resting in her femininity.
A Black woman who is soft, cared for, and allowed to breathe.

Not the strong one.
Not the dependable one.
Not the one everyone calls when life starts falling apart.

Just you.

If you're like many women reading this, that question made you pause.

Not because you don't know who you are.

And truthfully, some of you may need to dive a little deeper to rediscover who you are. That's okay too. We will walk through that together. I got you.

But somewhere along the way, you became responsible for being everything to everyone.

You became the fixer.
The problem solver.
The dependable one who can handle anything.

The strong one who holds everyone's feelings and emotions. The one who holds everything and everyone together, even when your own life feels like it is hanging on by a thread.

And let's be honest, friend. People have gotten comfortable with you being that woman.

Your family depends on it.
Your friends depend on it.
Your job definitely depends on it.

Sometimes it even feels like the entire world depends on Black women to fix what is broken.

But here is the truth we do not talk about enough.

Strength has quietly become a requirement.

Friend, for Black women, strength has never just been a choice. It has been survival.

We come from women who held families together, stretched what little they had, showed up when no one showed up for them, and still found a way to keep going.

That strength is real.

But it was never meant to cost us our peace.

Black women are always praised for being strong, resilient, and capable. Those are beautiful qualities to possess, but over time something else happens.

Strength stops being something we use when necessary and becomes something we are expected to carry at all times.

I do not know about you, but I have reached the point where I do not even like being referred to as strong anymore.

When people label you as strong, they often assume you do not need help. They assume you can handle everything on your own. They assume you will figure it out no matter what.

And, that expectation is exhausting.

Friend, you do not have to carry everything.

You were never meant to.

That expectation has created in Black women what I like to refer to as the Superwoman Complex.

The Superwoman Complex is the internal pressure many women feel to handle everything, solve everyone's problems, and never appear overwhelmed.

It convinces us that asking for help is a weakness. That resting is laziness instead of a necessity. That slowing down means we are falling behind.

So we push through exhaustion.

We silence our own needs.

We show up for everyone else while quietly hoping someone will notice we need support too.

Sometimes they do.

But many times they do not.

And when they do not notice, we start questioning ourselves.

Did I do something wrong?
Did I handle that the right way?
Should I have done more?

Not because people do not care.

But because we have become so good at wearing the cape that the world assumes we never need to take it off.

Now, before we go any further, I want to be clear about something.

This book is not about making Black women feel smaller or inadequate. Society does enough of that for us.

It is not about telling Black women to stop being strong, ambitious, capable, or successful.

Those qualities are part of our Black girl magic. It is what makes us special.

But somewhere along the way, they also became our burden.

This book is about removing the pressure to perform in strength all the time.

It is about recognizing that being powerful does not require you to carry the weight of the world alone.

History has always shown us examples of extraordinary Black women who displayed remarkable courage and strength.

A powerful example of that strength is Harriet Tubman.

She led hundreds of enslaved people to freedom, risking her life repeatedly in the process.

She was extraordinary.

But no one ever talks about the emotional stress and mental burdens and scars she carried while leading so many people to freedom.

She moved through fear, exhaustion, and danger, yet history remembers her strength more than her suffering.

And that pattern did not end with her.

You've seen it before. You know that woman.

The strength.
The composure.
The way she walks into a room and handles everything like it is light work.

Like Michelle Obama, graceful, poised, and unwavering under a level of scrutiny most people would crumble under. She carried a nation's expectations, raised her daughters in the public eye, supported her husband through history-making pressure, and still showed up polished. Behind that grace was discipline, sacrifice, and the constant demand to be everything to everyone without breaking.

Or Serena Williams, powerful, dominant, and seemingly unstoppable. The world watched her win, break records, and redefine greatness. What they did not always see were the injuries, the emotional strain, and the pressure of constantly proving herself while carrying both legacy and expectation.

And Phylicia Rashad, poised, graceful, and undeniably brilliant. She embodied excellence in a way that felt effortless, carrying herself with strength and dignity on and off the screen. Yet even in that grace, there is a story of discipline, expectation, and the quiet weight that comes with consistently showing up at the highest level.

And she is not alone.

There are countless other examples of women who consistently show up and give more than people expect, all while carrying it gracefully.

And that is where the Superwoman Complex begins to take shape.

Not in weakness, but in strength that becomes expected.
In excellence that becomes required.
In grace that is admired, but rarely supported.

It is the single mother who never lets her children see her cry.
It is the entrepreneur building something from nothing while smiling through uncertainty.
It is the woman holding her family together while quietly falling apart inside.

We have mastered the art of making strength look natural.
Of making heavy look light.
Of performing resilience so well that no one ever thinks to ask if we are okay.

But real strength was never meant to cost you your peace.

Over time, society began expecting everyday Black women to operate with that same level of unbreakable strength, all the time.

To keep going no matter what.
To carry everyone else's burdens.
To save as many people as we can.

But sis, that expectation is unrealistic.

As Black women in America, we are constantly tasked with fixing problems we did not create.

To save people who are not even trying to save themselves.

Friend, that is a lot to carry.

Mentally.
Emotionally.
Spiritually.

And if we are being honest in this moment, many of us are tired.

Not weak.
Not incapable.

Just tired.

Tired of being the strong one.
Tired of being the one who always has the answer.

Tired of being the one who keeps showing up while secretly wondering who is going to show up for us.

Friend, you do not have to carry everything.

If any part of that resonates with you, then this book is for you.

The goal of this book is not just to teach you how to remove the cape.

The goal is to rediscover the woman underneath it.

The woman who deserves rest.
The woman who deserves joy.
The woman who deserves support, softness, and peace.

And to remind you, you are still powerful without the cape.

In fact, you might discover you are even more powerful once you finally put it down.

So take a deep breath.

This book is not here to judge you.

It is here to free you.

So many of us have been wearing this cape for so long that we do not even remember what life felt like without it.

But before we talk about taking it off, we need to talk about how it got there in the first place.

Your Superwoman Complex did not appear overnight.

It was learned.
It was reinforced.

And for many of us, it started much earlier than we realize.

Let's talk about it.

Chapter One

The Cape We Never Asked For

Some roles we never chose. We just learned to carry them.

Friend, can I ask you something?

When did you decide you had to be strong all the time?

Not strong sometimes.
Not strong when life gets hard.

Strong all the time.

The one who figures it out.
The one who fixes the problems.
The one everybody depends on when things start falling apart.

Take a second and think about it, I'll wait.

For many of us, the Superwoman role began long before we even realized it was happening.

Where It Began

Sometimes it begins in childhood.

I know it did for me.

I am ten years older than my youngest siblings. Even when I was still figuring life out myself, I was already stepping into the role of the responsible one.

And if you are the eldest daughter, whew chile.

That is a conversation all by itself.

Somehow, the oldest daughter often becomes the second mother without anyone officially assigning her the job.

You help.
You step in.
You take responsibility.

Not because anyone forced you to.

But because it feels like the natural thing to do.

Looking back, my family never asked me to carry that level of responsibility.

I took it on myself.

And my friend, that is where the cape began in my life.

Not with some big dramatic moment.

But small expectations that slowly become part of who you are.

In many Black households, responsibility does not come with a conversation.

It comes with expectation.

You learn early how to help, how to adjust, and how to be strong, even when you are still trying to figure things out yourself.

And before you realize it, you are no longer just a child.

You are the one your family depends on.

When Responsibility Becomes Pressure

What starts as responsibility slowly turns into something else.

It turns into pressure.

Pressure to always show up.
Pressure to always be strong.
Pressure to always have it together.

And before you realize it, you are no longer choosing strength.

You feel required to perform in strength.

It Shows Up in Different Ways

Maybe your story looks different.

Maybe the cape showed up when you became the friend everyone calls for advice.

The one who listens.
The one who always knows what to say.
The one people turn to when they are going through something.

Or maybe it showed up with you being the unofficial group therapist.

When you began your career in corporate America you became the dependable coworker.

The one who gets the job done.
The one management relies on.
The one who stays late and makes sure everything runs smoothly.
The one last minute projects are passed to because they know you will get it done.

And let me be clear.

None of those things are bad.

Being dependable is beautiful.
Being responsible is admirable.
Being capable is powerful.

But when those qualities combine with constant expectation, something else quietly begins to happen.

You become the strong one.

Being strong stopped being something you did and became who you believed you had to be.

Once people start seeing you that way, it becomes very difficult for them to see anything else.

The Cost of Always Being Strong

Sis, let's be honest for a moment.

Being the strong one sounds good until it starts costing you something.

Your rest.
Your peace.
Your emotional well-being.

Because when you are always the one holding everything together, who is holding you?

When you are always the one showing up, when do you get to fall apart?

And if we are being real, most of us do not have the luxury of falling apart.

We keep going.
We keep pushing.
We keep smiling.

And we keep saying, "I'm fine."

Even when we are anything but.

This Isn't Just Personal. It's Cultural

For most Black women, strength was never optional.

It was modeled.
It was expected.
It was necessary.

We watched the women before us carry families, endure hardship, and keep moving no matter what.

We watched mothers, aunties, and grandmothers carry more than anyone should have to and still be expected to keep going.

So we learned to do the same.

And while that strength has carried us through so much, it has also quietly taught us to carry more than we were ever meant to.

That's the Cape

Think about it.

How many times have you been going through something difficult but still showed up for everyone else anyway?

How many times have you listened to someone vent about their problems while silently going through your own issues?

How many times has someone asked how you are doing, and your automatic response was, "I'm fine," even when you knew you were exhausted?

That is the cape.

The cape carries:

Pride.
Control.
Responsibility.
Guilt.
The pressure to be everything to everyone.

Sometimes the cape even convinces us we do not need help.

We start believing things like:

"I got it."
"I'll handle it."
"It's easier if I just do it myself."

But friend, you do not have to carry everything.

A Moment of Truth

Read this slowly.

You do not have to do everything.
You do not have to fix everything.
You do not have to be strong all the time.

You are allowed to need support too.

Your Body Knows Before You Do

Eventually, something inside you begins asking for something different.

Rest.
Support.
Space.
Peace.

And that quiet voice inside you is right.

Because no human being was designed to carry everything alone.

Sis Check-In

Before you move forward, pause for a moment and check in with yourself.

Take your time with these questions. There are no right or wrong answers here, just honest reflection.

When did I first start feeling like I had to be the strong one.
What responsibilities am I carrying that may not actually belong to me?
How often do I say "I'm fine" when I am actually overwhelmed?
When was the last time someone showed up for me the way I show up for others?

Sit with your answers.

Sometimes we do not realize how heavy the cape is until we stop long enough to notice everything we have been carrying.

And once you see it, you cannot unsee it.

You start noticing how often you show up for others while neglecting yourself.

You start noticing how quickly you say yes when you really need to say no.

You start noticing how uncomfortable it feels to admit you need help.

And that is when the real questioning begins.

Not just, "How did I get here?"

But, "Who have I become while carrying all of this?"

Because for many women, the cape does not just represent responsibility.

After a while, it becomes an identity.

So friend, let's talk about that next.

Chapter Two

When the Cape Becomes Who You Are

At some point, survival became identity.

We've talked about how the cape was formed.

How it started with responsibility.
How it grew through expectation.

But sis, it did not stop there.

After a while, the cape does not just sit on your shoulders.

It starts shaping how you see yourself.

Have you ever noticed how often people describe Black women as strong?

"You're so strong."
"You can handle anything."
"You always have it together."

At first, those words sound like compliments.
And in many ways, they are.

Strength is beautiful.
Resilience is powerful.

But over time, something subtle begins to shift.

Strength stops being something you use when life gets hard.
It becomes something people expect from you all the time.

Eventually, you begin to expect it from yourself.

And that is when the cape becomes more than something you wear.
It becomes part of who you believe you are.

And once it becomes who you are, you stop asking whether it is healthy, and start believing it is necessary.

And that's where it gets tricky.

When something becomes your identity, you stop questioning it.

You stop challenging it.

You simply accept it as who you are.

Why the Cape Feels Good at First

Let's be honest, sis.

Being the one who can handle everything feels good. At first.

People respect you.
They trust you.
They depend on you.

You feel capable.
You feel needed.
You feel important.

And for a while, that feels like power.

What we do not always realize is the power turns into pressure over time and the expectations of you become greater.

When Strength Becomes Identity

You become the strong friend.
The dependable daughter.
The responsible partner.
The one who always figures it out.

But here is something we do not talk about enough.

Those roles didn't just shape what you do.
They started shaping why you do it.

For some Black women, the cape does not just become identity.
It becomes protection.

For many Black women, the Superwoman Complex is not just something we internalize.

It is reinforced.

We are praised for being strong.

Expected to be unbreakable.

And denied the space to fall apart.

We are often given strength as identity before we are ever given space to be human.

So we learn to hold it all together, even when we need someone to hold us.

When the Cape Becomes Protection

Somewhere along the way, we learned that vulnerability was not always safe.

So we built armor.

We told ourselves:

"I'll handle it."
"I don't need help."
"I got this."

You convinced yourself you had it.

But friend, you do not have to carry everything.

And while that mindset may have helped you survive, survival strategies have a way of following you into seasons where you no longer need them.

Sometimes the cape becomes a security blanket.

A role you feel obligated to maintain.

Even when you are tired.
Even when you are overwhelmed.
Even when you wish someone would help you carry the weight.

And recognizing that truth might be the beginning of something new.

Let's Check In

Let's take this out of theory for a moment.

Because sometimes we do not realize how deeply rooted something is until we see it clearly.

Do You Have the Superwoman Complex?

Read each statement and answer Yes, Sometimes, or No.

- People regularly come to me for advice, emotional support, or solutions.
- I feel uncomfortable asking for help, even when I need it.
- I take on responsibilities because I believe things will not get done properly if I do not handle them myself.
- I push through exhaustion instead of resting.
- I feel guilty when I say no.
- I feel responsible for other people's happiness or emotional well-being.

- When someone asks how I'm doing, I say "I'm fine," even when I am overwhelmed.
- I struggle to delegate tasks or responsibilities to others.
- I feel like I have to hold everything together for the people around me.
- I rarely allow myself to be vulnerable or admit when I am struggling.

Quiz Results

If you answered Yes or Sometimes to more than half of these questions, there is a strong chance you are experiencing the Superwoman Complex.

And sis, if that realization makes you pause, you are not alone.

Many of us have been wearing the cape for so long that we do not even realize it is there.

But awareness is the first step toward putting it down.

The CAPE Framework

The Superwoman Complex does not show up in just one way.

It shows up in patterns.

I like to think of it as the CAPE.

C — Carrying Everything

You feel responsible for solving problems, managing situations, and holding everything together.

You become the one people rely on.

But friend, you do not have to carry everything.

A — Always Being Strong

You feel pressure to appear capable at all times.

You push through exhaustion.
You avoid vulnerability.

P — Perfection and Control

You believe things must be done a certain way, usually your way.

You struggle to delegate, so you carry it alone.

E — Emotional Labor

You become the emotional support system for everyone around you.

You listen.
You comfort.
You advise.
You absorb.

And over time, that emotional weight drains you.

If you saw yourself in more than one of these, that is not a coincidence.

That is a pattern.

The Hidden Cost of the Cape

The Superwoman Complex does not always show up in big moments.

It shows up in the small ones.

When you say yes but mean no.
When you take on something that is not yours.
When you carry emotions that do not belong to you.

At first, it feels manageable.

But over time, it becomes heavy.

You feel overwhelmed.
You feel drained.

You have been taking care of everyone else, but not yourself.

The Olivia Pope Effect

Sis, let's talk about something we all saw unfold in real time.

Shonda Rimes' fictional character, Olivia Pope.

She was brilliant.
Strategic.
Always in control.

She walked into chaos and made the impossible possible.

People trusted her to fix everything.

And she did.

But if you watched closely, you saw something else.

You saw the toll.
You saw the emotional weight.
You saw the unraveling.

Her relationships suffered.
Her peace was disrupted.

And if we are being honest, many of us saw ourselves in her.

Because the woman who fixes everything is rarely the woman someone checks on.

And sometimes the hardest part about wearing the cape is realizing no one is coming to save you.

Why Letting Go Feels So Hard

By now, you might be thinking, "If it is this exhausting, why do I keep doing it?"

Because the cape feels familiar.

It feels like control.
It feels like identity.
It feels like validation.

When people need you, you feel valuable.

But being needed and being supported are not the same thing.

Many women in our society are surrounded by people who need them, but not enough people who support them.

The Turning Point

This is where everything begins to shift.

Once you recognize the cape, once you understand how it formed, and once you see how it became part of who you are, you have a choice.

You can keep carrying it the way you always have.

Or you can start learning how to put it down.

Sis Check-In

Which part of the CAPE framework do I recognize most in myself?
Where in my life do I feel responsible for holding everything together?

When did being strong start to feel more like pressure than a choice?
What would it look like to let someone support me?
Do I believe I deserve help, or do I believe I should handle everything alone?

Take your time.

Because once you see it, you cannot ignore it.

And once you start noticing the cape, you begin to notice something else.

How often you are the one trying to fix everything.

Everybody's problems.
Everybody's emotions.
Everybody's chaos.

And sis, that habit deserves a conversation all by itself.

Chapter Three

Captain Save Everybody

You were never meant to fix everything.

Sis, can we be honest for a minute?

Everybody does not need saving.

And even harder to accept, everybody does not want to be saved.

I know that might not sit well at first.

Because if you are anything like me, helping people is second nature.

You see a problem, and you want to fix it.
You see someone struggling, and you want to step in.
You hear something that does not sound right, and your mind immediately starts creating solutions.

It is not coming from a bad place.

It comes from love.
From care.
From being the kind of woman who shows up.

But, that desire to help begins to turn into something else.

It can turn into a need to fix.

And sis, those are not the same thing.

The Two Roles We Play

When it comes to saving people, I have noticed women are the damsel or the savior.

No in between.

Some women want to be rescued.

They want someone to come in, take over, fix things, and make life easier.

They are comfortable receiving.
Comfortable being poured into.
Comfortable being supported.

And then there are women like us.

The ones who step in.
The ones who figure it out.
The ones who fix, solve, manage, and carry.

We become the ones people call when things fall apart.

The ones who make it happen.

The problem solvers.

We become Captain Save Everybody.

And most times we wear that title like a badge of honor.

We pride ourselves on being the one people can count on.

We tell ourselves:

"At least I'm helping."
"If I don't do it, who will?"

But sis, at what cost?

You cannot keep setting yourself on fire to keep everyone else warm.

Everybody Does Not Want to Be Saved

Can I let you in on a little secret?

Everyone is not looking for a solution.

Some people are comfortable in their chaos.
Some people are not ready to grow.
Some people do not want accountability.
Some people do not want to change.

They want to vent.
They want to repeat the same cycles.
They want to stay exactly where they are.

And when you step in trying to fix something they are not ready to change, it creates frustration.

Now you are investing energy into something that was never yours to carry.

Friend, that's exhausting.

You cannot rescue or heal someone who is committed to their habits.

You cannot fix someone who is comfortable in dysfunction.

And you cannot save someone who does not see themselves as needing to be saved.

When Helping Becomes Identity

For most of us, being the helper is not just something we do.

It becomes who we believe we are.

So when we cannot fix something, when we do not have the solution, or when someone does not take our advice, it makes us uncomfortable.

It can even make us feel less than.

Like, if I cannot help, what am I here for?

But sis, your value is not tied to your ability to fix things for other people.

You are valuable because of who you are.

Not because of what you carry.

This Runs Deeper Than We Think

For many Black women, this pattern is not random.

It is learned.

We watched women before us carry everything.

We watched them fix, hold, and manage entire households, relationships, and communities.

We watched mothers, aunties, and grandmothers show up no matter what they were going through.

We learned early that being the one who holds everything together is what makes you a "good woman" the "glue" if you will.

So we learned to do the same.

And while that strength is powerful, it also taught us something quietly.

That we are responsible for holding all the pieces together.

When No One Came to Save You

A lot of times the need to help comes from a deeper place.

There were moments in your life when you needed help, and no one came.

So you became the solution.

You became the strong one.

You told yourself you would never let someone feel the way you felt.

And that is beautiful.

But it cannot be the reason you keep overextending yourself.

Because giving from unhealed places will drain you.

Put your mask on first.

You have heard it before.

You absolutely, unequivocally cannot help anyone else if you are struggling to breathe.

But we check on everyone else first.

We fix everything first.

We carry everything first.

Friend, that is not smart nor is it sustainable.

Check Your Capacity

Before you help someone, ask yourself:

Do I have the mental or emotional capacity for this?

Not just time.

Because if you are already drained, what exactly are you pouring from?

You Are Allowed to Choose You

Choosing yourself is not selfish.

It is necessary.

You cannot keep abandoning yourself to prove your love for others.

The Shift

Helping others is not always the problem.

Overextending yourself is.

And once you understand that, everything begins to change.

A Simple Capacity Check

Before you say yes, ask yourself:

Do I have the mental space for this right now?
Do I have the emotional capacity for this?
Will helping them take away from something I need for myself?

If the answer is no, that is enough.

You can say:

"I love you, but I don't have the capacity right now."
"I care, but I need to take care of myself first."

You do not need to overexplain.

You just need to be honest.

Sis, Let's Check-In

Do I feel responsible for fixing other people's problems?
How do I feel when someone does not take my advice?
Have I been overextending myself trying to help people who are not ready to change?
Do I tie my value to how much I help others?
What would it look like to support someone without taking responsibility for them?

Take a moment and sit with your answers.

Sometimes we do not realize how much we have been carrying until we stop trying to carry everyone else.

And sis, once you stop trying to save everybody, you start noticing something else.

Everybody should not have the same level of access to you.

Not your time.
Not your energy.
Not your heart.

Chapter Four

The Circle of Trust

Not everyone deserves access to you.

Sis, let's talk about something that will change your life if you really take it seriously.

Who can you trust?

Not who you love.
Not who you've known the longest.
Not who you feel obligated to.

But who can you actually trust?

Because if we are going to talk about putting the cape down, we have to talk about the people standing around you when you take it off.

Trust Changes Everything

I believe the first step in putting away the Superwoman persona is evaluating the people in your life.

Because let's be honest.

If you do not trust someone, you are going to show up guarded.

You are going to hold back.
You are going to keep parts of yourself hidden.

You will smile.
You will show up.
You will play the role.

But you will not fully be yourself.

And that matters.

Because you cannot remove the cape in an environment where you do not feel safe.

Let's Talk About Trust

Now I know what people say.

"Love is given. Trust is earned."

And I am going to be honest with you, sis.

I do not fully agree.

I believe trust is given.

And when someone misuses that trust, then yes, it has to be rebuilt.

But starting every relationship with walls already up keeps you from experiencing real connection.

It keeps you in survival mode.

And we are not doing that anymore.

Define What Trust Looks Like for You

Here is where we have to get real.

Trust does not look the same for everyone.

What you consider trustworthy behavior might look completely different for someone else.

And that is where a lot of confusion in relationships comes from.

We assume people should just know.

We assume things should be understood.

But when you factor in upbringing, life experiences, emotional maturity, and cultural differences, what you see as disrespect might be a misunderstanding.

What you expect might not have been communicated.

And that is where unnecessary hurt comes in.

Open Your Mouth, Sis

Say what you need.

Communicate your expectations.

Tell people:

What you value.
What you need.
What you are willing to give.
What you are not willing to tolerate.

You set the tone for your relationships.

Not by controlling people, but by being clear.

Because unspoken expectations lead to unnecessary disappointment.

Removing the Mask

When you trust your circle, something beautiful happens.

You start removing the mask.

You stop pretending to have it all together.
You stop performing perfection.

You allow people to see the real you.

The you who gets tired.
The you who gets overwhelmed.
The you who needs support.

And if you never show that version of yourself, how will anyone know you need help?

They will not.

Because you have already been labeled as the strong one.

And sis, that label will have you suffering in silence if you let it.

Vulnerability Requires the Right Environment

Vulnerability and transparency are only as good as your circle of trust.

If you never reach a place where you feel comfortable sharing the hard things, you will always be seen as the reserved one.

The quiet one.
The one who does not need anything.

But sis, it is okay to not be okay.

And it is okay to let the right people see that.

Now hear me clearly.

Even within your circle, everyone will not have the capacity to hold all of your emotions.

That is not a reflection of your worth.

That is a reflection of their capacity.

And when you understand that, you stop taking it personally.

You start assigning people to the spaces they can handle.

And that clarity changes everything.

This Is Cultural Too

As Black women, we do not always grow up in spaces where vulnerability feels safe.

So we learn how to protect ourselves.

We become guarded, not because we want to be, but because we had to be.

We learn early that strength is expected, but softness is not always protected.

We learn how to hold it together in rooms where we cannot fall apart.

We learn how to smile through things we are still healing from.

And that makes trust feel complicated, even when we crave it.

When Someone Is Not Safe

Sis, let me say this clearly.

Everybody is not safe.

And I do not just mean physically.

Emotionally.
Mentally.
Spiritually.

Pay attention to how people handle:

Your vulnerability.
Your truth.
Your boundaries.
Your "no."

Do they listen or dismiss you?
Do they support you or compete with you?
Do they protect your confidence or repeat what you shared?
Do they show up consistently or only when it benefits them?

Because trust is not built on words.

It is built on patterns.

And if someone consistently shows you they cannot hold you properly, believe them.

Levels of Access

Not everyone gets the same version of you.

Friend, everybody cannot have the same level of access to you.

Not your time.
Not your energy.
Not your vulnerability.

Because when you give premium access to people who have not earned it, you end up drained.

Think of Your Life Like a House

Imagine your life like a house.

Everybody does not get a key.

Some people are on the porch.
Some are in the living room.
A few make it to the kitchen.

And only a select few enter your private spaces.

But many of us gave keys to people who never proved they could handle it.

And then wondered why we felt exposed.

That's why it's important to understand the different levels of access people have in your life.

Level One: Public Access

Acquaintances.

Surface conversations.

No emotional depth.

Level Two: Limited Access

Friends and extended connections.

You share, but with boundaries.

You are still discerning.

Level Three: Trusted Access

Your circle.

Consistent.
Supportive.
Safe.

Level Four: Sacred Access

Your inner circle.

The ones who see you fully and stay.

These people are rare.

And they should be.

Stop Overgiving to the Wrong Level

We give deep access too quickly.

And then feel hurt when it is mishandled.

But sis, they were never equipped for that level.

Access without discernment will always cost you.

Real Life Check

You share something personal.

Something you do not tell many people.

Later, you hear it repeated.

Casually.

Like it was never yours to protect.

Now you feel exposed.

Sis, that is not just a mistake.

That is a breach.

And that person just showed you what level they belong in.

Access Is Earned Through Consistency

Time does not equal trust.

Consistency does.

Character does.

Emotional safety does.

You Can Reassign Access

Hear me clearly.

Just because someone has had access to you does not mean they are entitled to keep it.

People can be reassigned.

Not out of anger.

But out of alignment.
Out of growth.
Out of self-respect.

And that is okay.

Protect Your Peace

When you assign the right levels, everything shifts.

You stop overgiving.
You stop overexplaining.
You stop overextending.

And you find peace.

Trust Requires Discernment

You are not required to open up to everyone.
You are not required to feel safe in every space.
Sometimes protecting your peace means choosing who gets access to you.
And that is not wrong. That is self-respect.

Sis Check-In

Who in my life do I genuinely trust?
Do I feel safe being vulnerable with the people around me?
Where am I overgiving access to people who have not earned it?
Have I ignored signs that someone was not emotionally safe?
Is there anyone I need to reassign in my life?
What would it look like to protect my peace without guilt?

Take your time with these questions.

And sis, once you understand who belongs in your circle, you begin to recognize something even deeper.

The difference between people who are around you and the women who are truly for you.

The ones who pour into you.
The ones who stand with you.
The ones who help you grow.

Let's talk about it.

Chapter Five

A Tribe Called Sisterhood

Strong women still need strong women.

Sis, I know what you might be thinking.

"Why is she talking about sisterhood? Isn't that the same as the circle of trust?"

And the answer is no.

Your circle of trust can include family, coworkers, acquaintances, and people you rely on in different areas of your life.

But your sisters?

That is different.

Your sisterhood is your lifeline.

These are the women who are irreplaceable.

The ones who see you, know you, and choose you.

The ones who give you roots and wings at the same time.

They hold you down when life feels heavy and push you forward when you forget who you are.

They are your safe place.
Your laughter.
Your truth.
Your people.

Friendship Changes as You Grow

When we are younger, friendship feels easy.

You meet someone, you connect, and just like that, she becomes your best friend.

There is less pressure.
Less discernment.
Less life experience shaping how you choose people.

But as we grow, something shifts.

We begin to understand ourselves more.

We begin to define our values.

We begin to decide what we will and will not accept in our lives.

And because of that, true friendship becomes harder to find.

Not impossible.

But intentional.

Because now, it is not just about who you like.

It is about who aligns.

Your Tribe Will Not Look Like Mine

Let's get this clear, sis.

Your sisterhood is not going to look like anyone else's.

And that is okay.

Every woman has different needs.
Different experiences.
Different seasons.

So the women in your life will reflect that.

You may have one friend you go to for advice.

Another you go to when you need to laugh.

Another who prays for you.

Another who tells you the truth, even when it is hard to hear.

And all of them matter.

Because no one person is meant to be everything for you.

But sometimes, you find that rare person who shows up in ways that feel like everything.

She is a gift.

And you are not meant to be everything for one person either.

You Cannot Do This Alone

Sis, let me say something that might challenge you.

You cannot fully remove the cape by yourself.

I know you have been doing everything on your own for a long time.

I know you have figured it out, pushed through, and handled things without help.

But healing in isolation only takes you so far.

At some point, you need people.

You need safe women.

And there is something sacred about Black women finding each other in safe spaces.

Because when we do, we finally get to exhale.

We do not have to explain ourselves.
We do not have to shrink.
We do not have to perform strength.

You get to just be.

And sis, you cannot build deep connection while constantly performing.

You need support.

Because the cape teaches you to do life alone.

Sisterhood reminds you that you do not have to.

It reminds you:

You are not by yourself.
You are not the only one.
You do not have to carry everything alone.

Be the Friend You Are Praying For

Now let's bring it back to you.

Before we ask, "Where are my people?" we have to ask:

Am I the kind of friend I am looking for?

Are you kind?
Are you patient?
Are you a good listener?
Are you loyal?
Are you trustworthy?

Because you cannot expect from others what you are not willing to give.

And I say that with love.

We all have areas where we can grow.

And sometimes building a strong sisterhood starts with becoming a better friend ourselves.

Start with the woman in the mirror.

Not All Sisterhood Is Healthy

Friend, let's be honest.

Every group of women is not sisterhood.

Some spaces look like connection but feel like competition.

Some relationships look like support but are filled with comparison, jealousy, and silent tension.

You will know the difference.

Real sisterhood feels safe.

It feels supportive.
It feels honest.

You can be yourself without feeling judged.

Fake sisterhood feels draining.

You feel like you have to perform.
You question where you stand.
You leave interactions feeling off instead of filled.

And if we are going to talk about removing the cape, you cannot do that in spaces where you do not feel safe.

Sisterhood Is a Safe Place

Your sisterhood should feel like a place where you can breathe.

Where you do not have to perform.
Where you do not have to pretend.
Where you do not have to carry everything.

These women will see you at your best and your worst and still choose you.

They will celebrate you when you win.

And they will sit with you when life does not go as planned.

They are your cheerleaders.
Your "yes and amen" corner.
Your "girl, don't do it" voices.

They will help you navigate life in ways that only women can truly understand.

Marriage.
Motherhood.

Career shifts.
Identity changes.
Health.
Life transitions.

And sis, that kind of connection is priceless.

It Takes Effort

Let's not skip over this part.

Sisterhood requires effort.

It requires time.
It requires consistency.
It requires showing up.

As we get older, life gets busy.

And if you are not intentional, friendships can fall to the side.

But if you want people to show up for you, you have to show up too.

Check in.
Make time.
Nurture the relationships that matter.

Because strong friendships do not just happen.

They are built.

Real Friendship Is Not Perfect

You will have disagreements.

You will have misunderstandings.

You might need space at times.

That is normal.

But real sisterhood comes back together.

It communicates.
It grows.

It does not run at the first sign of discomfort.

Because it understands the value of what it holds.

When You Feel Like You Do Not Fit

To the woman who says,

"I do not get along with other women."
Or
"Women just do not get me."

Sis, I hear you.

But I am also going to challenge you.

Look inward.

Sometimes it is not "other women."

Sometimes it is past hurt.
Sometimes it is trust.
Sometimes it is how you show up.

Healing those areas creates space for connection.

Because women are necessary.

They are your sounding board.
Your support system.
Your safe place through seasons others may not understand.

And you deserve that.

Building Your Tribe Intentionally

If you do not currently have the sisterhood you desire, that does not mean it is not available to you.

It just means you have to be intentional.

Start small.
Be open.
Be kind.
Be consistent.

Show up in spaces where alignment exists.

And most importantly, be yourself.

Because the right people are not looking for perfection.

They are looking for authenticity.

And when you find your people, you will feel it.

Your Sisters Will Check You

A real sisterhood will not just comfort you.

It will correct you.

They will tell you when you are doing too much.

When you are overextending.

When you are putting the cape back on.

They will remind you:

They will tell you to rest.

To choose yourself.

To put your mask on first.

And sometimes, they will be the ones who show up for you in ways you did not even realize you needed.

Sisterhood Is What You Need

When you feel like you are drowning trying to be everything to everyone, your sisters will be the ones who understand.

The ones who help you breathe again.

The ones who help you navigate difficult waters.

They will laugh with you.
Cry with you.
Pray with you.
Push you.
Love you through every version of yourself.

And sis, that kind of support is not optional.

It is necessary.

Sis Check-In

Do I currently have women in my life who truly support me?
Am I showing up as the kind of friend I desire?
Am I open to building deeper connections with other women?
Have past experiences affected how I view sisterhood?
Am I in spaces that feel safe or draining?
What would it look like for me to intentionally build or strengthen my tribe?

Take your time with these questions.

Sometimes the life you are praying for is connected to the people you allow into your life.

And sis, this is what sisterhood is meant to feel like.
Not pressure. Not performance. Not carrying everything alone.

It is support.
It is honesty.
It is space to be fully yourself without having to prove anything.

Real sisterhood reminds you that you do not have to be everything.
You just have to be you.

Let's talk about it.

Chapter Six

Jill of All Trades Syndrome

Doing everything is not the same as doing what matters.

Sis, can we talk?

Because this right here?

This might hit a little different.

When was the last time you sat down and did nothing?

Not scrolling your phone.
Not answering emails.
Not thinking about your next task.

Just nothing.

If you had to think about it too long, that tells me everything I need to know.

Because somewhere along the way, friend, you got used to being busy.

Not just busy but responsible for everything.

You're feeding the baby
throwing clothes in the dryer

answering texts
giving advice
handling work
keeping everything moving

All at the same time.

Jill of All Trades, Master of None

Are you the woman who can do all of that at once?

Be honest.

Because if you are, you've probably worn that like a badge of honor.

And let's acknowledge it.

That level of multitasking?

That takes skill.

That takes awareness.

That takes capacity.

But sis, let's talk about the other side of that.

Just because it works in real time does not mean it's working for you.

Because what looks like productivity on the outside, can quietly be draining you on the inside.

You're moving fast.
You're getting things done.
You're checking boxes.

But your mind is split in five different directions.

Your energy is stretched thin.

And your body?

It's keeping score.

Friend, doing everything at once might make you feel efficient, but it's often detrimental to your health.

Mentally.
Emotionally.
Physically.

I know as Black women we have mastered doing everything.

Handling work.
Handling home.
Handling emotions.

Often without acknowledgment, without rest, and without support.

And somewhere along the way, we started believing that doing it all was normal.

So let me ask you something real.

Why are you trying to do everything at the same time?

Is it because you feel like you have to?

Is it because slowing down feels uncomfortable?

Or did you learn somewhere along the way that being busy makes you valuable?

Sis we need to challenge that.

Because the Superwoman Complex will have you believing that the more you do

the more you matter.

And that is simply not true.

Why You Keep Doing Everything

This didn't just happen overnight.

You didn't wake up one day and decide to do everything for everybody.

You learned it.

You adapted to it.

You survived through it.

At some point, doing everything became your default.

Because if you didn't do it

it didn't get done.

If you didn't step in, things fell apart.

If you didn't show up

no one else did.

So you learned:

"I'll just handle it."

And over time

that became your default.

But just because something is familiar

does not mean it's healthy.

Friend, you don't have to carry everything.

The Illusion of Productivity

Let's call it what it is.

A lot of what we think is productivity, is actually overextension.

You're doing a lot.

But are you doing what actually matters?

Or are you just staying busy so you don't have to slow down?

Because slowing down requires you to sit with yourself.

And for many of us

that feels unfamiliar.

So instead

we stay moving.

We fill our schedules.
We fill our time.
We fill our energy.

Even when we are completely drained.

Sis, productivity is not about how much you can do.

It's about doing what actually matters.

Let's Talk About Control

Some of what you're carrying?

Is not just responsibility.

It's control.

Because sometimes it's not that nobody else can do it

it's that they won't do it the way you would.

And that discomfort?

Makes you step in.

Again and again.

But friend, trying to control everything

will keep you exhausted.

Because control says:

"If I don't do it, it won't be right."

But peace says:

"It doesn't have to be perfect to be done."

Prioritize and Eliminate

Let's simplify this.

Not everything deserves your time.

Not everything needs your attention.

Not everything belongs on your to-do list.

Some things need to be prioritized.

The things that actually matter.
The things that require your presence.
The things that align with your life in this season.

And some things?

They need to be eliminated.

Not because they're bad.

But because they're unnecessary.

Because they add to the illusion of your busyness, without adding value to your life.

And sis, let's be honest.

A lot of what we're doing isn't essential.

It just feels important because we're used to being in motion.

But constant motion is not the same as meaningful progress.

Your Body Is Not Built for Constant Go

Did you know your body was not designed to stay in "go mode" all the time?

Always thinking.
Always doing.
Always anticipating the next thing.

That's survival mode.

And when your body stays there too long, it starts responding.

Fatigue.
Irritability.
Brain fog.
Emotional exhaustion.

Your body is not failing you.

It's trying to get your attention.

Rest is not optional, it's necessary.

Living Within Your Capacity

Sis, let me introduce you to something we don't talk about enough.

Capacity.

Not what you *can* do.

But what you can do well

without draining yourself.

Because there is a difference.

You can push yourself past your limits.

You've done it before.

But that doesn't mean it's sustainable.

And it definitely doesn't mean it's healthy.

Less Is More

Doing less might actually give you more.

More peace.
More clarity.
More energy.
More presence.

Because when you stop trying to do everything, you honor your capacity and create space for what actually matters.

And what matters is You, friend! You matter.

Daily Reset Routine

Because slowing down has to be intentional.

And it's not about becoming a completely different woman overnight.

It's about creating small moments where you stop performing and start choosing yourself.

1. Morning Check-In

Before you reach for your phone

pause.

Ask yourself:

How do I feel today?
What do I actually have the capacity for today?
What matters most today?

2. Pick Your Top Three

Instead of trying to do everything

choose three things that truly matter.

That's it.

3. Build in Pause Moments

Friend, you need space in your day.

Even if it's five minutes.

Sit.
Breathe.
Reset.

You don't have to earn rest.

4. Evening Release

At the end of the day, let it go.

Not everything will get done.

And that's okay.

You showed up.

And that is enough.

Sis Check-In

Where in my life am I doing too much?

What am I holding onto that I can release?

Do I feel guilty when I rest?

Am I trying to control outcomes instead of allowing support?

What would it look like for me to operate within my capacity?

Take your time.

Because this is where the shift begins.

Sis,
you are not behind.

You are not failing.
You are not dropping the ball.

You are simply learning that doing everything was never the goal.
Managing your capacity was.
Focusing on what actually matters was.

Because trying to do everything at once is not productivity.
It is overload.

Multitasking has been your default.
But doing more does not mean you are doing what matters.

Friend, this is your invitation to slow down.
To choose what deserves your time.
To honor your capacity instead of pushing past it.

Because it is one thing to recognize you are doing too much.
It is another thing to do less on purpose.

And girlfriend,
that is where things really start to change.

Let's talk about it.

Chapter Seven

Little Miss Perfect

Looking put together is not the same as being whole.

Girlfriend, let's talk about Little Miss Perfect.

You know exactly who I'm talking about.

Her hair is always done.
Her nails are always done.
Her clothes are always laid.

Everything about her presentation is on point.

She walks into a room and people notice.

She looks like she has it all together.

She moves like she has it all together.

And if you asked anyone on the outside, they would say she does.

But sis, let's go a little deeper.

Because Little Miss Perfect is not just about appearance.

It is about control.

It is about performance.

It is about maintaining an image that says:

"I've got it."

Even when she does not.

The Performance of Having It Together

Friend, there is a version of the Superwoman Complex that does not look stressed.

It does not look overwhelmed.

It does not even look tired.

It looks polished.

It looks composed.

It looks like everything is exactly how it should be.

But behind those looks, there is pressure.

Pressure to maintain the image.
Pressure to never slip.
Pressure to always be on.

Because the moment something feels out of place, she feels it.

Not just externally, but internally.

And if we are being honest, that level of perfection is exhausting.

Why Perfection Feels Safe

Let's go even deeper.

Perfection is not just about how things look.

It is about safety.
You learned that:
If everything is in order, you are okay.
If everything looks right, you are accepted.
If everything is handled, nothing can fall apart.

For many Black women, being put together is not just preference.

It is an expectation.

So you tightened your grip.

On your image.
On your life.
On yourself.

Because control felt safer than uncertainty.

And perfection felt safer than vulnerability.

But what protects you can also trap you.

When Perfection Becomes Identity

Little Miss Perfect does not just like things done well.

She needs them to be.

Because being put together stopped being a choice and became part of who she is.

She is the one who always has it together.

The one who does not drop the ball.

The one who makes everything look easy.

But sis, easy and effortless are not the same thing.

What looks effortless on the outside often requires constant effort behind the scenes.

And that effort adds up.

The Woman Who Never Sat With Herself

Sometimes perfection becomes armor.

Because if everything looks right on the outside, no one questions what you are carrying on the inside.

So you stay polished.

You stay ready.

You stay on.

Because slowing down might reveal something you have not made space for.

How tired you really are.

How much you are carrying.

How much of your life is performance instead of presence.

Sis, that is a hard truth.

When the Image Starts to Crack

And let's be real, friend.

There comes a moment when keeping it all together starts to feel like too much.

You are still showing up.

Still polished.

Still put together.

But underneath that, you are tired.

Not the kind of tired that sleep fixes.

The kind that comes from holding it together for too long.

And in those quiet moments, you start asking yourself:

"How long can I keep this up?"

When Image Matters More Than Truth

How much of your life is about how things look versus how they actually feel?

Because everything can look perfect and still not feel right.

You can look good and still feel overwhelmed.

You can have it together and still feel disconnected.

You can be admired and still feel unseen.

You can look perfect and still be exhausted.

That is the trap.

Because the image gets validated.

But the woman underneath it gets ignored.

The Hidden Weight of "Having It All Together"

Sis, maintaining perfection is heavy.

Keeping everything in order is heavy.

Always showing up polished is heavy.

And the truth is, eventually, it will wear you down.

Because no one can perform perfection forever.

At some point, something has to give.

And for many women, it is not the image.

It is them.

Letting Go of the Performance

Friend, you do not have to perform your life.

You do not have to look perfect to be worthy.

You do not have to have it all together to be valuable.

You do not have to maintain an image to be loved.

And more importantly, you do not have to carry everything behind the scenes just to keep the front looking good.

Sis, perfection is just another version of the cape.

It just looks prettier.

You Are Allowed to Be Human

You are allowed to have an off day.

You are allowed to not have it all together.

You are allowed to be seen without everything being perfect.

You do not lose your value when things are messy.

You do not lose your worth when you need help.

You do not lose who you are when you stop performing.

You simply become more honest.

Try This

I want you to try something this week.

Do one thing imperfectly on purpose.

Leave something undone.

Ask for help.

Show up without over-preparing.

And instead of fixing it, sit with it.

Because that discomfort is where freedom starts.

Sis Check-In

Am I more focused on how my life looks than how it actually feels?
Do I feel pressure to always appear put together?
When was the last time I allowed myself to not have it all together?
What am I afraid would happen if I let people see the real me
Do I feel safe being seen without the "perfect" version of myself?

Take your time with these.
Because this chapter is about honesty.

Sis, you do not have to be perfect to be whole.
You do not have to have it all together to be worthy.

Because the pressure to look like you have everything under control is part of the cape too.

Once you start letting go of that pressure, you are going to run into something else.

Boundaries.

Because you cannot maintain an image and protect your peace at the same time.
At some point, you have to choose.

Let's talk about it.

Chapter Eight

No Is Your Superpower

What you protect determines how you live.

Sis, let's talk about something that sounds simple but feels incredibly hard.

No.

Such a small word.

But for so many of us, it feels heavy.

Uncomfortable.

Even wrong.

Because somewhere along the way, we learned that saying yes made us good.

Helpful.
Dependable.
Needed.

So we said yes.

Yes when we were tired.
Yes when we were overwhelmed.
Yes when we really wanted to say no.

And over time, that yes became automatic.

Friend, let me ask you something.

How many times have you said yes when your spirit was screaming no?

That tension you feel in those moments is not random.

That is your body trying to tell you something.

Why No Feels So Hard

Saying no is not just about the word.

It is about what we believe will happen after we say it.

We worry people will be disappointed.

We worry we will be seen differently.

We worry we will no longer be needed.

And if we are being honest, sometimes we worry that saying no makes us less valuable.

For many Black women, that feeling runs even deeper.

Because we have been taught, directly and indirectly, that our value is tied to how much we can do for others.

We are expected to show up.
To carry.
To handle.

So we say yes.

Not always because we want to.

But because it feels like who we are supposed to be.

What Saying Yes Has Cost You

Sis, let's be honest for a moment.

Saying yes all the time comes with a cost.

It costs you your energy.
It costs you your peace.
It costs you your time.

Sometimes it even costs you yourself.

Because every time you say yes when you really mean no, you abandon your own needs.

And over time, that builds resentment.

Not just toward others.

But toward yourself.

Every yes to others should not come at the expense of you.

What No Actually Means

No is not rejection.
No is not disrespect.
No is not you being difficult.

No is clarity.

No is self-respect.

No is you honoring your capacity.

When you say no, you are not taking anything away from someone else.

You are giving something back to yourself.

What No Looks Like

Let's make this practical.

Because sometimes we know we need to say no, but we do not know how.

No can sound like:

"That doesn't work for me."
"I'm not available for that."
"I can't commit to that right now."
"I need to sit this one out."

Simple.

Clear.

Complete.

No explanation required.

When You Need a Firm No

Sis, sometimes it is not about being gentle.

Sometimes you need to be clear.

"I said I'm not available."
"That's not something I'm willing to do."
"I need you to respect that decision."

No softness.

No over-explaining.

Just truth.

What No Is Not

No is not rude.
No is not selfish.
No is not unkind.

And no is not something you have to soften with a long explanation.

Because when you over-explain, you are not setting a boundary.

You are asking for permission.

And you do not need permission to honor yourself.

What Saying No Looks Like in Real Life

Let's bring the concept of no into your everyday life.

Because this is where it really matters.

Saying no to family might look like:

Not answering every call immediately.
Not taking on responsibilities that are not yours.
Choosing rest instead of showing up out of obligation.

Saying no at work might look like:

Not overcommitting just to prove yourself.
Not taking on extra tasks when your plate is already full.
Leaving work at work instead of carrying it home.

Saying no in friendships might look like:

Not always being the one who shows up when you are drained.
Not being the emotional dumping ground for everyone else.
Being honest when you do not have the capacity.

Saying no does not mean you do not care.

It means you care about yourself too.

No Does Not Require Agreement

People do not have to agree with your no for it to be valid.

They may not understand it.
They may not like it.
They may push back.

And that does not mean you are wrong.

Your no is not up for debate.

The First Time You Say No

Sis, the first time you really say no, it is going to feel different.

Your voice might shake.

You might feel uncomfortable.

You might replay the conversation in your head afterward.

That is okay.

You are not doing it wrong.

You are doing something new

Learning to Say No Without Guilt

Friend, this is where the real work begins.

Because saying no is one thing.

Saying no without guilt is something else entirely.

At first, it will feel uncomfortable.

You may second-guess yourself.

You may feel like you should explain more.

You may feel like you should go back and say yes.

Do not.

That discomfort is not a sign that you did something wrong.

It is a sign that you are doing something different.

And different takes practice.

You Are Not Responsible for Everyone

You are not responsible for everyone.

Not for their emotions.
Not for their decisions.
Not for fixing every situation.

That is not your assignment.

And just because you have the ability to help does not mean it is your responsibility to do so every time.

What You Are Really Saying Yes To

Sis, every time you say no to something that drains you, you are saying yes to something that restores you.

Yes to your peace.
Yes to your time.
Yes to your energy.

And that matters.

Because your life is shaped by what you say yes to.

A Moment of Truth

Where in your life are you saying yes out of obligation instead of alignment?

Sit with that.

Sis Check-In

Where am I struggling to say no?
What am I currently saying yes to that is draining me?
Do I feel guilty when I choose myself? Why?
What would it look like for me to honor my capacity more consistently?
What am I afraid will happen if I start saying no more often?

Take your time with these

Because this is where your boundaries begin.

Sis, every no you give someone else is a decision to choose yourself again.

Chapter Nine

Boundaries Are a Form of Self-Respect

What you allow will continue.

Sis, now that we have talked about saying no, we need to talk about what actually holds that no in place.

Boundaries.

Because saying no is powerful, but without boundaries, you will say no today and then turn around and say yes tomorrow.

And if we are being honest, friend, we have all been there.

You finally say no.
You feel good about it.

Then someone pushes back, and suddenly you are explaining, adjusting, or giving in.

Sis, that is not a boundary.

That is a suggestion.

What Boundaries Really Are

Girlfriend, let's clear something up.

Boundaries are not walls.
They are not about shutting people out.
They are not about being cold or distant.

Boundaries are standards.

They are the lines that define what you accept, what you tolerate, and what you are no longer available for.

And most importantly, they are how you teach people how to treat you.

Because whether you realize it or not, people are always learning you.

They learn what you allow.
They learn what you tolerate.
They learn how far they can go with you.

And if there are no boundaries, they will keep going.

For many of us, especially as Black women, boundaries were not modeled.

We watched women give, give, and give without stopping.

We watched them carry everything without complaint.

So now we are learning in real time what it means to protect ourselves without feeling guilty about it.

When Boundaries Do Not Exist

Let's tell the truth, friend.

When boundaries do not exist, we overextend ourselves.

We say yes when we mean no.
We tolerate behavior that does not feel good.
We keep showing up in spaces that drain us.

We ignore our feelings.

We silence our needs.

We stretch ourselves thin trying to keep everything and everyone together.

Then we wonder why we feel overwhelmed, resentful, and exhausted.

Sis, it is because you have been living without boundaries.

Access without boundaries will always lead to burnout.

Types of Boundaries

Let's bring some clarity here, because not all boundaries look the same.

Emotional boundaries protect what you take on and what you do not.
Just because someone shares something with you does not mean you are responsible for carrying it.

Time boundaries protect how your time is spent.
Everyone does not get unlimited access to your time, and everything is not urgent.

Energy boundaries protect what drains you and what restores you.
Some spaces, conversations, and people will pour into you, while others will take from you.

Relational boundaries protect how you show up in your relationships with family, friends, and partners. They define what you are available for, what you will no longer tolerate, and how you expect to be treated.
Not every relationship requires the same level of access, and not every person is entitled to all of you.

When you understand the different types of boundaries, you begin to see exactly where you have been overextending yourself.

Boundaries Protect Your Peace

Let me say this clearly.

Boundaries are not punishment.

They are put in place as a form of protection.

They protect your time.
They protect your energy.
They protect your mental and emotional well-being.

And most importantly, they protect your peace.

Because without boundaries, anything and anyone can access you.

Why Boundaries Feel Uncomfortable

Even when you know you need to set boundaries for yourself, it can still feel very uncomfortable.

You might feel guilty.
You might feel like you are being mean.
You might worry about how people will react.

That discomfort is real.

But just because something feels uncomfortable does not mean it is wrong.

It means you are doing something different.

And different will always feel unfamiliar at first.

You Cannot Have Boundaries and People-Pleasing at the Same Time

You cannot have strong boundaries and still be committed to people-pleasing.

At some point, you have to choose.

Because people-pleasing says, "Keep them happy."

But boundaries say, "Honor yourself."

And those two things do not always align.

Boundaries Require Consistency

And here is where most will struggle.

Consistency.

Setting a boundary one time is easy.

Holding that boundary is where the work is.

People will test it.

Not always intentionally, but they will.

They will ask again.
They will push a little more.
They will see if you really mean what you said.

In that moment, you have to decide.

Am I going to stand on what I said, or am I going to fold?

Because every time you fold, you teach people your boundary is flexible.

Boundaries Without Consequences Do Not Work

Friend, let's take this a step further.

A boundary without a consequence is just a conversation.

If someone crosses your boundary and nothing changes, the behavior will continue.

Not because they are trying to hurt you.

But because there is no reason for them to adjust.

Consequences do not have to be dramatic.

Sometimes it looks like:

You stop engaging.
You remove access.
You create distance.
You follow through.

That is what makes a boundary real.

What Boundaries Look Like in Real Life

Let's make this practical.

You stop answering calls or texts immediately when you need space.
You leave conversations that feel draining.
You stop over-explaining your decisions.
You stop saying yes out of obligation.
You stop tolerating behavior that makes you uncomfortable.

Not aggressively.

Not disrespectfully.

But clearly.

Because clarity is kindness, to yourself first.

What Boundaries Sound Like

Sometimes you just need the words.

"I am not available for that."
"That does not work for me."
"I need to step away."
"I cannot commit to that."
"I am choosing something different right now."

Short.

Clear.

Direct.

When You Don't Honor Your Own Boundaries

Sometimes it is not other people crossing your boundaries.

Sometimes it is you.

You say you are tired, but you keep saying yes.

You say you need space, but you keep showing up.

You say something does not feel right, but you ignore it.

That is you abandoning yourself.

And friend, that is where the real work begins

Because people will treat you based on what you allow.

But you will experience life based on what you tolerate.

Boundaries and Relationships

Friend, boundaries will always reveal things.

They will show you who respects you, who listens to you, and who honors your space.

They will also show you who does not.

And that can be hard.

Because sometimes the people who struggle with your boundaries are the ones who benefited from you not having them.

But that does not mean your boundaries are wrong.

It means things are changing.

You Are Allowed to Choose You

You are allowed to choose yourself.

You are allowed to say:

"This does not work for me."
"I am not available for that."
"I need space."

Without guilt.

Without over-explaining.

Without shrinking.

And you do not have to make yourself uncomfortable to keep others comfortable.

Sis Check-In

Where in my life do I lack boundaries?
What am I currently tolerating that does not feel good?
Do I struggle with being consistent when I set boundaries?
Am I afraid of how people will react if I change?
Where have I been ignoring my own needs?
What would it look like for me to protect my peace daily?

Take your time with these.
Because this is where your life begins to shift in a real way.

Sis, what you allow will continue.
But what you choose to honor will begin to change everything.

Because setting boundaries is not just about saying no.
It is about respecting yourself.
It is about honoring your capacity.
It is about creating space for who you are and what you need.

And friend, when you start setting boundaries, you are advocating for yourself in a way you may not be used to.
You are choosing your peace.
You are choosing your time.
You are choosing yourself.

And in that choice, you create something powerful.

You create space.
Space to rest.
Space to breathe.
Space to take care of yourself.

And that brings us to something we do not talk about enough.

Self-care.

Let's talk about it.

Chapter Ten

Self-Care Is Not a Luxury

Rest is necessary, not a reward.

Sis, let's have a real conversation.

Self-care has been misunderstood for far too long.

We started calling things like spa days, vacations, and getting our nails done "self-care."

And do not get me wrong, those things are nice.

But that is not the kind of self-care that sustains you.

Real self-care is deeper than that.

It is not just how you look.

It is how you live.

What Self-Care Is Not

Self-care is not avoidance.
It is not distraction.

Scrolling for hours is not self-care.

Ignoring your needs is not self-care.

Overworking and calling it discipline is not self-care.

Self-care is not about escaping your life.

It is about building a life you do not need to escape from.

What Are You Saying Yes To This Week?

What are you saying yes to this week?

And just as important, what are you saying no to?

Maybe your yes sounds like:

"I am saying yes to being present with my children."
"I am saying yes to resting when my body is tired."
"I am saying yes to myself."

And maybe your no sounds like:

"I am saying no to unnecessary screen time."
"I am saying no to overextending myself."
"I am saying no to things that drain me."

Sis, that right there is self-care.

Because self-care is not always about adding more.

Sometimes it is about removing what no longer serves you.

Why We Neglect Ourselves

Many of us were not taught to take care of ourselves.

We were taught to take care of everyone else.

To show up.
To be strong.
To keep going.

For many Black women, that expectation runs deep.

We learned early how to give.

How to show up.

How to carry.

Even when no one was checking if we were okay.

So when it is time to choose ourselves, it feels unfamiliar.

And sometimes, it even feels selfish.

But sis, taking care of yourself is not selfish.

It is necessary.

Self-care is not always soft.
It is not always pretty.
It is not always easy.

Self-care is heart work.
And heart work is hard work.

Because it requires you to look at yourself honestly.
To sit with yourself.
To ask yourself questions you may have been avoiding.

Heart work also looks like accountability and grace.
Accountability for your choices, your patterns, and the ways you show up.
Grace for the version of you who did the best she could with what she knew at the time.

And sometimes, it may require more.
It may require seeking therapy for past trauma and pain.
It may require doing the deeper work to understand why certain things happened the way they did,
and how those experiences shaped who you are today.

Who am I right now?
Do I like the woman I am becoming?
Am I living in alignment with my truth?

That kind of reflection can be uncomfortable.
But it is necessary.

Becoming Someone New

If this season has given us anything, it has given us perspective.

It has forced many of us to slow down.

To look at ourselves from the inside out.

To evaluate who we are and where we are.

For some of us, that reflection has been painful.

But it has also been powerful.

Because growth requires honesty.

Sis, you are not the same woman you were months ago.

And that is okay.

That means you are evolving.

That means you are becoming.

And becoming requires grace.

What have you done for yourself lately to help you evolve?

Balance Versus Harmony

We hear the word balance all the time.
Work-life balance.
Life balance.
Trying to juggle everything evenly.

But let's tell the truth.
Balance can feel exhausting.

Because balance makes you feel like everything has to get equal attention.
And that is not realistic.

Instead of balance, focus on harmony.

Harmony means everything works together.
Not equally, but intentionally.

Harmony also looks like honoring the natural rhythms in your life,
instead of trying to keep all the balls in the air at once.

There will be times you are saying yes to one thing
and no to other things.

And you have to be okay with what that looks like.

Some days your focus will be your family.
Some days your focus will be your work.
Some days your focus will be you.

And that is okay.

Harmony allows your life to shift without guilt.

Less Is More

Sis, let's simplify this.

You do not need to do everything.

You do not need to be everywhere.

You do not need to carry everything.

Less is more.

Less pressure.
Less overthinking.
Less overcommitting.

Because when you remove the unnecessary, you create space for what actually matters.

And sometimes, self-care looks like doing less on purpose.

Being Allowed to Breathe

Friend, when was the last time you allowed yourself to breathe?

Not rushed breathing.
Not survival mode.

Real, intentional stillness.

Self-care looks like rest.
It looks like a pause.
A moment to simply breathe.

When was the last time you truly inhaled and exhaled?

Many of us have been living in constant motion.
Always moving.
Always thinking.
Always doing.

And we forgot how to just be.

Sis, you are allowed to breathe.
Not because everything is done.
But because you deserve it.

The CARE Method

When you think about self-care, remember this.

CARE.

C — Check in with yourself
How do I feel? What do I need right now?

A — Acknowledge your limits
You are not unlimited. Honor your capacity.

R — Release what is not yours
Not every responsibility belongs to you.

E — Engage in what restores you
Choose what actually fills you back up.

This is how self-care becomes a lifestyle.

Self-Care in Small Moments

Self-care does not have to be big.

It can be small.

Saying no to one thing.
Taking five minutes to breathe.
Putting your phone down.
Choosing rest instead of pushing through.

Small choices create real change.

A SWOT Analysis of Your Life

Let's take the concept of self care a little deeper.

You may have heard of a SWOT analysis in business.

Strengths.
Weaknesses.
Opportunities.
Threats.

But have you ever applied that to your life?

Your strengths may be the very things people rely on you for.

Your ability to listen.
Your ability to show up.
Your ability to carry others.

But those same strengths can become your weaknesses if they are not managed.

Being the strong one can make you feel like you cannot be vulnerable.

Being the listener can make you absorb everyone else's emotions.

Being dependable can make you feel like you cannot rest.

That is why boundaries and self-awareness matter.

Your opportunities are the things you desire.

Growth.
Peace.
Joy.
Expansion.

But if you are not intentional, you can begin attaching yourself to other people's visions and forget your own.

And your threats?

Sometimes it is not other people.

Sometimes it is you.

Your habits.
Your patterns.
Your resistance to rest.

Sis, self-care requires you to be honest about all of it.

So take a moment and ask yourself:

Where am I operating from strength and where am I operating from survival?

Living Within Your Biorhythms

Let's talk about something we often ignore.

Your natural rhythm.

Your body tells you when it needs rest.

Your mind tells you when it needs a break.

Your spirit tells you when something is off.

But many times, we override those signals.

We push through exhaustion.

We ignore fatigue.

We keep going when we should be resting.

Then we wonder why we feel depleted.

Self-care is listening to your body.

It is honoring your limits.

It is respecting your rhythm.

Self-Care Is Discipline

Self-care is not indulgence.

It is discipline.

It is choosing yourself daily.

Even when it is inconvenient.

Even when it is uncomfortable.

It is saying no when you need to.

It is resting when your body asks you to.

It is creating space for yourself without guilt.

That is real self-care.

You cannot pour from a place you refuse to replenish.

A Moment of Truth

Sis, you have taken care of so many people.

When was the last time someone took care of you and you actually allowed it?

Sis Check-In

What am I currently saying yes to that is draining me?
What do I need to start saying no to immediately?
Am I giving myself space to grow and evolve?

Do I feel balanced, or do I need to create harmony?
When was the last time I truly rested without guilt?
Am I living in alignment with who I am becoming?

Take your time with these.

Because this is where healing begins.

Sis, the life you want will require a version of you that knows how to rest, receive, and reset.

And that version of you starts with how you take care of yourself.

Once you begin to take care of yourself differently, you start to see yourself differently.

You begin to redefine what strength really looks like.

Because strength is not just about what you can carry.

It is also about what you are willing to release.

Let's talk about it.

Chapter Eleven

Your Power Was Never the Problem

You just have to learn how to use it.

Sis, let's clear something up.

Your power has never been the problem.
It was never your strength.
It was never your ability to handle things.
It was never your capacity to show up.

The problem was never that you are powerful.
The problem is how you have been using that power.

Because you started using your strength to carry everything, fix everything, and be everything to everyone.
And in doing that, you exhausted yourself.

But friend, your power was never meant to drain you.
It was meant to support you.

Do Not Be Afraid of Your Superpowers

Sis, every woman has power.

Your intuition.
Your resilience.

Your ability to adapt.
Your ability to lead, nurture, and create.

Those are not small things.
Those are superpowers.

The question is not whether you have them.
The question is how you are using them.

Are you using your power to pour into yourself?
Or are you using it to constantly pour into everyone else?

Because power without direction will always lead to exhaustion.

Every Woman Has Power, But She Must Learn How to Use It

Just because you can do something does not mean you should.

You can handle everything.
You can figure it out.
You can make things happen.

But at what cost?

Friend, part of your growth is learning restraint.
Learning when to step in.
And learning when to step back.

Because real power is not about doing everything.
It is about choosing what actually deserves your energy.

Just because you are strong does not mean everything is yours to carry.

What Using Your Power Actually Looks Like

Using your power is not always loud.

Sometimes it looks like:

Choosing rest instead of proving a point.
Not answering the call when you need space.
Letting people figure things out on their own.
Walking away from what no longer aligns.

Power is not always in what you do.
Sometimes it is in what you choose not to do.

Power Versus Performance

There is a difference between being powerful and performing power.

Performing power looks like always having it together.
Always showing up.
Always being the strong one.

But real power is quiet.
It is intentional.
It is rooted.

It does not need to prove anything.

Sis, you do not have to prove your strength anymore.
You have already survived enough to know who you are.

Stay Ready So You Don't Have to Get Ready

So let's reframe what it actually means to be ready.

What are you doing to make sure you are ready?

Not for everyone else.
For yourself.

Because the Superwoman Complex will have you constantly preparing to show up for everyone else,
while quietly neglecting what you need.

Are you taking care of your mental health?
Are you protecting your peace?
Are you building habits that support your life?

Because staying ready is not about being in constant motion.
It is about being aligned.

So when opportunities come, you are not scrambling.
You are prepared.

Not because you forced it.
But because you have been pouring into yourself consistently.

Imposter Syndrome and the Alter Ego

Let's talk about something real.

Imposter syndrome.

That feeling that you do not belong.
That you are not qualified.
That you are not enough.

We have all felt it at some point.

And for many women, especially those carrying the Superwoman Complex,
that feeling does not always show up as shrinking.

Sometimes, it shows up as overcompensating.

Doing more.
Proving more.
Trying to be everything so no one ever questions your worth.

But what if, instead of overextending yourself, you leaned into a different version of yourself?

Not a fake version of you.
A focused version of you.

The version of you that trusts herself.
The version of you that moves with confidence.
The version of you that does not overthink every step.

Sis, that woman is already inside of you.

Stepping Into Her On Purpose

As you become a softer version of yourself,
you begin to release the version of you who felt like she had to control everything and carry it all.

You know she is still inside of you.
The woman who no longer leads with pressure, but with peace.

She is not rushing.
She is not overextending.
She is not trying to prove anything.

She is choosing herself.
She is honoring her capacity.
She is moving with intention instead of pressure.

You do not have to become her overnight.
You just have to start choosing her daily.

One decision at a time.

Laying Down the Cape

And as you begin choosing her, you will start laying the cape down.

Not all at once.
Not perfectly.
But intentionally.

There will be moments when you feel the urge to pick it back up.

Moments when it feels easier to go back to what you know.
To step in.
To fix it.
To carry it.

Because that version of you is familiar.

But sis, just because you can pick it back up
does not mean you have to.

Because now, you have something you did not have before.

Awareness.
Boundaries.
Discernment.

You know how to pause.
You know how to say no.
You know how to recognize what is not yours to carry.

And when the moment comes, and it will,
you respond differently.

You breathe.
You assess.
You choose.

Because laying down the cape is not a one-time decision.
It is a daily choice.

Perfection Paralysis

Friend, can we talk about something else that keeps you stuck?

Perfection.

Perfection will have you waiting.
Waiting for the perfect moment.
Waiting until everything is just right.
Waiting until you feel fully ready.

And in the meantime, nothing moves.

That is perfection paralysis.

It looks responsible.
But it is fear.

Because the truth is, you do not need perfect.
You need progress.

Final Truth

Friend, this is where everything comes together.

You are powerful.
That is not changing.

But how you use that power is everything.

You can use your power to overextend yourself,
to carry everyone,
to drain yourself trying to be everything.

Or you can use your power
to set boundaries,
to choose yourself,
to build a life that actually feels good to live.

Sis, your power has never been the problem.
Misuse is.

So let me ask you something.

Are you tired because life is heavy?
Or because you have been carrying things that were never yours to hold?

Sit with that.

Because you are not losing anything by putting the cape down.
You are gaining yourself back.

Sis Check-In

Am I afraid of my own power?
How am I currently using my strengths?
Am I using my power to support myself or to carry others
Where am I waiting for perfection instead of taking action?
What would it look like for me to trust myself fully?

Take your time with these.

Because this is where your confidence begins to grow.
This is where you learn that power is not just something you have.
It is something you steward.
It is something you direct.

Sis, your power is not something you need to shrink.
It is something you need to use wisely.

Removing the cape was never about becoming less.
It was about becoming more of who you truly are.
A woman who knows her strength.
A woman who honors her capacity.
A woman who understands that real power is not in carrying everything.
It is in knowing what is yours and what is not.

And the truth is, life is still going to ask things of you.
People will still need things.
Opportunities will still come.

But now the question is different.

Not, "Can I handle it?"
You already know you can.

The real question is:

Is this the best use of my power?
Is this mine to carry?
Does this align with the life I am building?
Am I choosing this, or am I defaulting to who I used to be?

Because how you answer those questions
will determine the version of you that shows up next.

And that, sis, is power.

Chapter Twelve

Living My Life Like It's Golden

Ease is not something you earn. It is something you allow.

Sis, take a deep breath.

You made it here.
Not just to the end of this book, but to a new understanding of yourself.

Something shifted.

Maybe you realized how heavy the cape has been.
Maybe you admitted you were tired.
Or maybe you finally gave yourself permission to choose differently.

Whatever it was, you are not the same woman who started this journey.

The Cape Is No Longer Required

You have carried enough.

You have proven your strength.
You have shown your resilience.

Now it is time to release the cape.

Not because you are weak.
But because you are wise.

Strength does not require constant sacrifice.
And power does not require constant exhaustion.

You Do Not Have to Earn Rest

You do not have to earn rest.
You do not have to prove you are tired enough.

Rest is not a reward.
It is a necessity.

And once you accept that, everything begins to shift.

A Life That Feels Different

Imagine a life where you are not overwhelmed.
Where you are not carrying everyone else's weight.
Where you can breathe without guilt.

A life of ease.
A life of peace.
A life with space.

Space to rest.
Space to think.
Space to simply be.

And in that space, you are still loved.
Still valued.
Still enough.

Not because of what you do.
But because of who you are.

A Life Where Your Magic Can Breathe

You are magic.

Black Girl Magic to be specific.

But your magic was never meant to live in survival mode.

It was meant to expand.
To breathe.
To exist without constant pressure.

Because it cannot shine when you are depleted.
It cannot grow when you are overwhelmed.

But when you give yourself space, your energy shifts.

You become more grounded.
More present.
More aligned.

And most importantly, sustainable.

You Can Be Supported and Still Be Powerful

You can be supported and still be powerful.
You can rest and still be successful.
You can receive and still be in control.

You do not have to do everything alone.

Real strength is knowing what to carry
and what to release.

Choosing a Different Life

This is where your life begins to change.

Not the life where you are constantly proving yourself.
But the life where you are intentional.

A life where:

You say no without guilt.
You rest without explanation.
You choose yourself without hesitation.

And in that life, you lose nothing.

You gain everything.

Take It Off

Picture yourself holding the cape you have carried for years.

The expectations.
The pressure.
The responsibility.

Now make a decision.

Take it off.

Not because you cannot carry it.
But because you no longer need to.

This Is What Freedom Looks Like

You move differently now.

You pause before you say yes.
You honor your capacity.
You choose peace over pressure.

And your life does not fall apart.

It gets better.

A Moment With Yourself

Who are you becoming?
What are you no longer willing to carry?
What does your life look like without the cape?

Take your time.

This is not just reflection.

This is transformation.

Your New Truth

I do not have to carry everything.
I am allowed to rest.
I am allowed to receive.
I am still powerful without the pressure.

Final Sis Check-In

What does a life of ease look like for me?
Where can I create more space right now?
What am I ready to release?
Do I believe I am worthy of rest, peace, and support?
What does it look like to live freely as myself?

There are no wrong answers.

Only truth.

From Me to You

I wrote this because I understand.

I know what it feels like to carry everything.
I know what it feels like to be the strong one.

And I know what it feels like to finally put it down.

You deserve that too.

You are allowed to live a life that feels good.
Not just looks good.

You were never meant to survive your life.
You were meant to live it.

Final Close

You were never meant to carry everything.

You were meant to live.
To love.
To grow.
To experience joy without exhaustion.

You do not have to pick the cape back up.
Not tomorrow.
Not next week.
Not ever.

Because the woman you are becoming does not need it.

She is still powerful.
Still capable.
Still enough.

You are still her.

You are just no longer carrying what was never yours.

And that is what it looks like to live your life like it's golden.

Acknowledgments

To the women who believed they had to be everything.

The strong one.
The dependable one.
The one who never breaks.

To the women who felt invincible, unstoppable, and necessary in every space.

I see you.

But sis, even Superwoman gets tired.

The cape is heavy.

And you do not have to carry it forever.

Remove it when you are ready.

You are enough, even without the cape.

Ashley Alridge

About the Author

Ashley Alridge is an author and speaker who is passionate about helping women live with clarity, harmony, and intention.

Ashley is deeply committed to encouraging mothers to embrace purpose beyond the demands of motherhood. As a mother of two boys, she understands the balance of nurturing others while still honoring who you are as a woman, and she believes both can exist without compromise.

Through her writing, Ashley creates space for women to release pressure, rediscover themselves, and build lives that feel as good as they look.

When she is not working or writing, Ashley enjoys creating memories with her family and friends, getting lost in good books, binge-watching great shows, and trying new restaurants.

Made in the USA
Coppell, TX
16 June 2026

81353076R00085